PRAISE FOR YOUR INTELLECTUAL PROPERTY FORTRESS

Zara and Sean are the only intellectual property attorneys I trust! They have so much wisdom and experience and never waste a moment protecting your business. This book is the gateway to truly owning your brand and your future wealth.

Chelsya Ashley
Agency Owner of Cheya Media and Host of Seven Figure Diaries™
www.cheyamedia.com

Zara and Sean's legal prowess made our trademarking process seamless. Your Intellectual Property Fortress is the essential guide for innovative entrepreneurs looking to navigate the intricacies of trademark law. With real-life anecdotes and expert tips, this book is a must-have resource in protecting your brand.

Tiffany Howard and Tiffany Lewars, Co-Founders
Vows of Style
www.vowsofstyle.com

We love referring clients to Zara and Sean because they make protecting your business feel simple, strategic, and totally doable. This book breaks down exactly how to safeguard your business like the asset it truly is-clear, actionable, and a must-read for every entrepreneur.

Hannah Wardenburg and Alexandra Markulis, Co-Founders
The Wealth Collaborative
www.thewealthcollaborative.co

Your Intellectual Property Fortress" is a must-have. Zara and Sean are not only exceptional attorneys, but guides who walk beside you along the path to securing your currency, and ultimately, your dreams.

Dr. Laura Eustache Zamor, BCDN, CHHP
Author, The Whole Mother Method ™

YOUR INTELLECTUAL PROPERTY FORTRESS

The Ultimate Guide to Protecting Your Brand and Business from Copycats

Zara Young, Esq. and Sean Young, Esq.

JT PUBLISHING HOUSE

Your Intellectual Property Fortress
Copyright © 2025 by Zara Young, Esq. and Sean Young, Esq.

Names: Young, Zara and Young, Sean.
Title: Your/ Zara Young and Sean Young.

Summary: "Your Intellectual Property Fortress: The Ultimate
Guide to Protecting Your Brand and Business From Copycats is the essential
playbook for powerhouse women entrepreneurs scaling high-end brands in
coaching, fashion, beauty, wellness, and lifestyle. "— Provided by author.

Identifiers: ISBN 1-9781954624-25-2 (paperback)
ISBN 978-1-954624-30-6 (ebook)
ISBN 978-1-954624-27-6 (hardback)

Subjects: BISAC: LAW / Intellectual Property / Trademark

Library of Congress Control Number: 2025910868

Published by JT Publishing, Spartanburg, South Carolina
www.jtpublishinghouse.com

Printed in the United States of America
10 9 8 7 6 5 4 3 2 1

DISCLAIMER

A NOTE ABOUT CLIENT STORIES

The stories and case studies shared throughout this book are based on real client experiences. In every instance, we've obtained permission to share these stories. Some client names and identifying details have been changed to protect privacy and maintain confidentiality, while others appear with consent and reflect their actual names and brand journeys.

These stories are included for educational purposes and to illustrate common challenges and legal principles that apply to brand protection and trademark law. They're not intended to serve as legal advice or a substitute for professional counsel tailored to your specific situation.

TABLE OF CONTENTS

DEDICATION

To our beloved daughters, Victoria and Chloé, may you always dream boldly, fearlessly, and with limitless imagination.

INTRODUCTION

THE NAME THAT BUILT AN EMPIRE THEN DISAPPEARED

"A wise man builds his house upon a rock."
—Matthew 7:24

What began as a creative outlet quickly became Samantha's full-time business. She poured everything into growing her jewelry brand, taking it from her kitchen table to a thriving online store in just two years, all without the protection of a registered trademark. She built a brand people trusted. A name that meant something.

Until the day it didn't.

The email came in quietly. Subject line: Cease and Desist.

She stared at her screen, the air thick with panic. Someone else had claimed legal ownership of her brand name. They had the trademark. She did not.

Within days, her website was taken offline. Her social media accounts were flagged. Her loyal customers were confused. And the name she had built an entire identity around?

Gone.

Not because she wasn't talented. Not because she didn't work hard. But because she didn't own the rights to her name.

Samantha's story isn't a cautionary tale from the margins, it's a wake-up call for anyone building a business in today's crowded marketplace.

Because here's the truth: if you don't legally own your brand, you're building on borrowed ground.

THE POWER BEHIND YOUR NAME

A name is never just a name. It's your first impression, your reputation, your story. It holds your vision and reflects your values.

Throughout history, names have carried meaning and power. In many ancient cultures, a name wasn't simply a label. It was an identity. For example, the Hebrew word for "name," Shem, translates to "being." Your name reflects your very being, who you are at your core.

Your business name is no different.

It tells the world what you stand for. It connects your mission to your market. And when you build a brand that people love, your name becomes one of your most valuable business assets. But here's what too many entrepreneurs don't realize: if you haven't trademarked it, you don't fully own it.

WHAT YOU DON'T PROTECT, YOU COULD LOSE
Imagine this...you spend years building a recognizable brand. You refine your visuals, shape your messaging, and grow a loyal customer base. Then, a competitor enters the market with a similar name, and the confusion begins.

Your sales are slow. Your reputation suffers. You start fielding customer emails asking if you've been bought out or, worse, if you're the copycat. And without a registered trademark, you have no legal footing to fight back.

This doesn't only happen to business owners who aren't serious. It happens to those who are. Those who put everything into building a brand but unwittingly leave its legal foundation exposed.

Big brands don't make that mistake. Apple. Chanel. Nike. They don't simply create, they protect. They register trademarks. Monitor for infringement. Enforce their rights. Because they know your brand is only as strong as your ability to defend it.

WHO WE ARE
We're Zara and Sean Young, a husband-and-wife legal team and the founders of Watson & Young. We built our law firm from the ground up with a single mission: to help female founders own, honor, and protect what they've built.

Over the years, we've worked with thousands of business owners—from boutique startups to global brands—to secure their trademarks and safeguard their legacies. Our clients are trailblazers. Women who are building businesses that reflect their brilliance, courage, and calling.

We understand what it takes to bring a vision to life and what it costs to lose it.

We've seen too many female founders forced to rebrand, re-strategize, or rebuild because they skipped the legal foundation. Not because they weren't capable, but because no one told them how high the stakes really were.

That's why we do this work. Protecting your brand isn't just about legal filings, it's about securing your future. It ensures that what you've built remains yours, whether you choose to pass it down, scale it, or sell it one day.

WHY THIS BOOK EXISTS

Ideas are currency. But in today's business world, currency without protection is easy to steal. An idea alone isn't enough—it's the execution, the branding, the consistency, and the recognition that transform it into real value. And at the heart of that value is your intellectual property.

Your brand is how the world knows you.

But recognition without legal protection is risky. That's where this book comes in.

This is your go-to guide for protecting your brand before someone else tries to claim it.

Whether you're launching your first business, scaling a fast-growing brand, or laying the groundwork for an eventual exit, this book is your blueprint for securing your name, your reputation, and your legacy.

14

We'll walk you through the exact legal steps to trademark your business name, lock down your brand assets, and build a legal fortress around everything you've worked so hard to create.

Trademarks don't just shield you from legal battles. They open doors to new opportunities. They increase your business's valuation. They help you license, collaborate, scale, and sell with confidence. They give you leverage. They give you peace of mind. They give you power.

So, what exactly is a legal fortress?

It's the invisible, yet unbreakable, structure surrounding your brand. Every trademark you file, every asset you protect, every right you enforce, these are the bricks that build that fortress.

It keeps opportunists out. It makes your business harder to copy, easier to trust, and more valuable in the eyes of investors, customers, and partners. Without that fortress, your business is exposed. With it, your brand becomes untouchable.

This book is designed to give you protection, confidence, and control.

You'll learn how to:
- Understand what makes a name legally protectable.
- Register trademarks the right way.
- Avoid common legal pitfalls that derail growth.

- Recognize infringement and take action.
- Use your intellectual property as a business asset.

Whether you're at the beginning of your journey or years into the business you've built, this is your legal roadmap to protecting your brand at every stage.

Let's make sure no one else gets to write your story.

CHAPTER 1

IS YOUR BRAND AT RISK? WHAT MOST ENTREPRENEURS MISS (UNTIL IT'S TOO LATE)

"By wisdom a house is built, and through understanding it is established; through knowledge its rooms are filled with rare and beautiful treasures."
— Proverbs 24:3-4

The digital age has seen a major shift when it comes to protecting brands—both our own and those of our clients.

When we first launched our firm in 2017, the idea of a law firm operating primarily online was still pretty unheard of. Most people associated lawyers with traditional office spaces, where you'd sit across from your attorney in a conference room filled with stacks of legal books. So, when we explained that our firm would operate virtually, we were often met with blank stares and skepticism.

We remember those reactions clearly—other attorneys looked at us like we were crazy. But we knew something they didn't: technology was revolutionizing how business operated, and we had an opportunity to serve clients in a way that was more accessible, efficient, and modern. Instead of being confined to a physical office, we built a digital-first law firm designed to protect brands in a fast-moving, online world.

If you're serious about building and growing a business today, embracing technology isn't a choice—it's a necessity. Every successful business today has a strong digital presence—it's the foundation of growth and visibility. But with greater visibility comes greater responsibility.

The internet is like the wild, wild west. It's exciting, full of opportunities, but also unpredictable. To truly thrive, businesses must take charge of protecting what they've built. Without legal protection, your brand is vulnerable to being copied, misused, or even stolen by competitors looking for shortcuts.

SEO, PAID ADS, AND THE POWER OF LEGAL PROTECTION
A big part of being visible in today's market is making sure people can find you. Our client, advertising and marketing coach, Ashley Brock, even coined the phrase Become Findable™ to highlight just how crucial it is to make your business easy to discover. Ashley teaches business owners how to use paid advertising to reach the right audience, helping them get noticed and attract customers who are ready to buy.

As the author of *How to Win with Paid Ads*, Ashley simplifies the process so entrepreneurs can confidently increase their visibility and attract the right clients. Her proven strategies have helped countless business owners grow their revenue and stand out in a crowded market.

But here's the catch: when you become more visible, you also become more vulnerable.

The more people who see your brand, the greater the risk that someone might try to copy it.

And in today's digital-first world, visibility is the foundation of business growth. That's why business owners invest in strategies like Search Engine Optimization (SEO) and Google Ads. These are two of the most powerful tools for getting in front of the right audience. But what most entrepreneurs don't realize is that increased visibility also means increased risk.

Take SEO, for example. When someone searches for your business online, you want to rank at the top. SEO helps improve your website's positioning so more potential customers can find you organically.

But what if a competitor starts using your brand name in their website content or metadata to appear alongside or even above you in search results? Without legal protection, you may have little recourse to stop them from profiting off the brand identity you worked so hard to build.

Then there's paid advertising. Many business owners use Google Ads to secure top placement in search results when potential customers are looking for their products or services. Others leverage Meta Ads (on Facebook and Instagram) and YouTube Ads to reach highly targeted audiences.

But here's what many don't realize—competitors can bid on your brand name across these platforms. That means when someone searches for your business on Google, scrolls Instagram, or watches a related video on YouTube, they might see a competitor's ad first redirecting potential clients away from you.

Here's where trademarks come into play. If you don't have a registered trademark, there's not much you can do to prevent others from using your name in their marketing. But when you own the trademark for your brand, you have the legal right to stop competitors from using it in their ads, SEO strategies, and online content.

Think about it like this: if you rented a storefront and spent years building a loyal customer base, how would you feel if a competitor set up shop right next door, using a name nearly identical to yours? They'd intercept your foot traffic, confuse customers, and likely steal sales. The same thing happens online every day with Google Ads and SEO. That's why trademark protection isn't just a legal formality. It's a business necessity.

Another area business owners often overlook? Domain names and social media handles. Imagine pouring your heart into growing your brand, only to find that someone else has registered a website with your name or grabbed your Instagram handle before you could.

Customers searching for you could easily end up in the wrong place, mistaking an imitator for the real thing. With a trademark, you gain the leverage to claim these spaces and prevent others from misusing your name.

Take one of our past clients as an example. Joan ran a successful branding and design studio. One day, during a routine Google search, she came across another business using the exact same name. What made matters worse?

This other business had recently expanded from offering only copywriting services to now providing branding and website design, which directly overlapped with Joan's offerings.

When we ran a search on Google, we noticed that the competing business appeared first in the search results. This posed a serious risk of consumer confusion. Potential clients could easily assume the two brands were the same, which they absolutely weren't.

Because Joan had a registered trademark, we were able to step in. We sent a cease and desist letter demanding that the other business change its name. This is a prime example of why digital visibility and trademark protection go hand in hand.

Another client story illustrates this even further. One of our clients created a fun and unique fitness program that took off on TikTok.

Her videos went viral, and the program quickly became a trend. She was even interviewed on national television about it. Her brand was everywhere.

But that visibility came at a cost. As soon as she gained traction, major fitness companies and popular influencers started using her program's name to promote their own content. Some even created similar offerings based directly on her concept without giving her credit or asking for permission.

Her visibility opened the door to incredible opportunities, but it also exposed her brand to copycats. That's the part many business owners don't expect: once your ideas are out in the world, especially in a digital space, others may try to capitalize on them. If your brand isn't legally protected, it's easy for others to benefit from what you built.

Thankfully, we worked with her to secure trademark protection in the right categories, giving her the legal tools to defend her brand and preserve her growing momentum.

Visibility is powerful, but it also comes with responsibility. The more attention your brand attracts, the more important it becomes to ensure it's legally protected.

From our experience, people who copy don't always do it maliciously. Many act out of fear, uncertainty, or simply a lack of awareness around intellectual property law. They see a successful brand and assume they can follow the same blueprint without understanding the legal consequences. People often say, "Imitation is the sincerest form of flattery." But in business, it's not flattery—it's a threat.

Copycats can dilute your brand, confuse your

audience, and impact your revenue. And in a fast-moving digital world, it's easy to feel overwhelmed by the idea of protecting everything you've created.

But here's the truth: no matter your industry, whether it's wellness, education, coaching, or marketing, your brand is yours, and it deserves to be protected.

Protecting your brand is about ownership. It's about making sure that what you've built stays in your hands. The good news?

You don't have to do it alone. Securing trademarks, monitoring your digital presence, and staying informed are key steps in safeguarding your business and building with confidence.

If you're building something meaningful, don't wait. Take the right steps to protect it. Your brand is your legacy. You must nurture it, safeguard it, and let it thrive.

In the next chapter, we'll break down one of the most common myths in business, one that gives a lot of entrepreneurs a false sense of security. If you think your brand is fully protected just because you've registered your business, it's time for a closer look. What you don't know can hurt your brand.

CHAPTER 2

HOW ICONIC BRANDS ARE BUILT: WHY MOST ENTREPRENEURS GET IT WRONG

"A good name is rather to be chosen than great riches, and loving favour rather than silver and gold."
—Proverbs 22:1

In a world that moves fast and forgets even faster, how do you create something that lasts?

Think about the brands that still inspire us decades later—Chanel, Ford, Disney. Their names aren't just known; they're trusted, remembered, and respected. They've become part of our culture, our language, and even our family stories.

That kind of staying power doesn't happen by accident. It's the result of strategy, clarity, and protection. And if you're building something that matters, your name deserves the same level of care.

Chanel, Gucci, Hermès, Versace, Dior, Ford, Ferrari, Rolls-Royce, and Walt Disney are all examples of brands named after their founders. Their names didn't survive by chance; they were protected by intentional legal strategy and reinforced through generations of brand stewardship. Today, they don't just represent excellence, success, and legacy. They prove that true brand longevity demands more than creativity; it demands protection.

Ford is synonymous with innovation in cars.

Chanel is synonymous with luxury, quality, and timelessness.

These brands have become status symbols and are worth billions. The emotional connection that customers have with brands like these is immeasurable.

Now, think about your brand. Is it something you want to pass on to future generations or perhaps sell one day?

Regardless of your goals, your business name and brand assets, including logos, slogans, and designs, are valuable assets that should be treasured, honored, and protected. They are forms of intellectual property that can be passed down in a will or trust or even sold as valuable assets.

Protecting them helps ensure that the name and vision you've worked so hard to create will live on and continue to have value.

How Brands Transcend Generations

Some brands, like Disney or Ford, have stayed within families or been entrusted to new leadership while staying true to their original mission. How do they do it? By creating systems and processes that ensure the brand's core values remain intact. Here are practical steps you can take to help your brand live on:

1. **Define Your Purpose:** Write a mission statement or brand manifesto that outlines your purpose, vision, and core values. Share it with your team so everyone understands what your brand stands for and why it matters.

2. **Build a Consistent Identity:** Create a brand style guide with rules for logo usage, colors, typography, tone of voice, and messaging. Update it as your brand evolves, but always stay true to your original identity.

3. **Document Your Processes:** Develop clear step-by-step procedures for essential areas like marketing, customer service, and hiring. Ensure these processes reflect your brand values, making it easier to train new team members and stay aligned with your mission.

4. **Hire Aligned People:** Your team is the face of your brand. Hire people who share your vision and values. Use onboarding programs to immerse them in your brand's culture and teach them how to uphold its mission.

5. **Conduct Regular Brand Audits:** Take time to evaluate your marketing, products, services, and customer feedback to help make sure they still reflect your mission. Adjust when necessary but stay true to your brand's heart.

Passing Down vs. Selling Your Brand

If you're planning to pass your brand to your family, start by teaching them its values and vision. Make them a part of the journey and show them how to uphold your legacy. As a business owner, what you're really passing down to your children is education, skills, and values. You're passing down an education in perseverance, entrepreneurial skills, and the values that built the business in the first place. Your brand becomes more than a business; it becomes a powerful symbol of your family's work ethic and commitment to making an impact.

Involve your children early. Show them how decisions are made, why customer relationships matter, and how to protect the heart of a brand. At the time of this writing, our two daughters are five and two years old. They are tiny witnesses to the dreams we're building and the values we're living.

Each day, as they watch us nurture and protect our business, they're learning lessons that extend far beyond entrepreneurship: resilience, vision, and the importance of building something that lasts. In many ways, building our brand is as much about their future as it is about ours.

We're intentionally instilling these values early, knowing that even if they choose different paths one day, they'll carry forward the understanding of what it means to create, protect, and honor a legacy.

On the other hand, if you're considering selling, know that protecting your intellectual property, like trademarks, copyrights, and patents, can significantly increase your brand's market value. During a business deal, what you're truly offering to buyers isn't just your products, services, or physical assets. It's your intellectual property, the unique identity, and ideas that set your business apart.

PREPARING YOUR BRAND FOR SALE

Deciding to sell your business is a big step, and making sure it's ready for the next chapter can be both emotional and empowering. Your goal isn't just to attract buyers. It's to honor everything your brand represents and set it up for continued success.

Here are some practical ways to prepare:

1. **Conduct an IP Audit:** Think of this as checking the roots of your brand's foundation. Make sure your trademarks, copyrights, and patents are properly registered and up to date so they can support the future of your business.

2. **Strengthen Brand Recognition:** A brand that's well-loved and respected is a gift to both buyers and the customers they'll continue to serve. Invest in marketing that connects with people and builds trust, so your legacy feels alive and thriving.

3. **Create a Brand Portfolio:** Imagine this as a scrapbook of your brand's journey. Compile your logos, slogans, designs, and even trade secrets into a well-organized collection that

shows how much value your business holds.

4. **Streamline Operations:** Buyers are drawn to businesses that run smoothly. Take the time to document your processes and refine how things work so your brand's next owner can step in with confidence.

5. **Build Financial Transparency:** Clear and honest financial records aren't just numbers—they're proof of your brand's success. Share the story of your profitability and the revenue your intellectual property generates to showcase its true worth.

CREATING A WILL FOR YOUR BRAND

Your brand represents your hard work, creativity, and vision. It's an essential part of the legacy you'll leave behind.

Whether it's your name, logo, or the unique ideas that define your business, these assets deserve to be carefully protected and prepared for the future.

Here's how you can protect your brand's future:
1. **Identify Your Brand's Key Assets:** Make a detailed list of your brand's trademarks, copyrights, logos, slogans, designs, and other valuable intellectual property. These elements can be transferred to your heirs or managed effectively after your lifetime.

2. **Include Your Brand in a Will or Trust:** Work with an attorney to have your brand's assets legally included in your estate plans. A trust is particularly valuable because it can provide ongoing management of royalties or other income your brand generates while keeping your plans private. Unlike a will, which becomes public during probate, a trust keeps your estate details confidential.

3. **Appoint a Responsible Caretaker:** Choose a person or organization you trust to manage your brand's operations or protect its value. Clearly outline your expectations so your brand continues to reflect your vision.

1. **Establish Management Guidelines:** Create clear instructions for how your brand should be used and maintained. Consider setting up licensing agreements or other tools to guide its use and preserve its reputation.

2. **Review and Update Regularly:** As your business evolves, update your estate plans to reflect new trademarks, branding assets, or changes in your goals. This keeps your plans relevant and effective.

Including your brand in a will or trust allows it to remain a protected and valuable asset, capable of supporting your loved ones or continuing its impact in the hands of the next generation.

Planning now not only secures your legacy but also provides peace of mind, knowing your efforts will endure.

LICENSING AND MONETIZING YOUR LEGACY

Licensing is a powerful way to keep your brand active and thriving while still maintaining ownership. By granting others the right to use your intellectual property, like your brand name, logo, or designs, you can expand your reach, generate additional income, and protect the integrity of your brand.

Well-known brands like Marvel and Star Wars have achieved massive growth through licensing. From merchandise to media partnerships, these brands have created new opportunities for success while retaining control over their identity and vision. Similarly, Chanel has extended its luxury appeal worldwide by licensing perfumes and beauty products, maintaining its exclusivity while tapping into new markets. Ralph Lauren, known for its sophisticated lifestyle branding, has successfully licensed home goods, fragrances, and accessories to transform its name into a global powerhouse.

Here's how you can use licensing to grow and monetize your brand:

1. **Identify What to License:** Determine which elements of your intellectual property—such as your name, logo, slogans, or product designs—are most valuable and marketable. Focus on assets that align with your vision and have strong potential to attract partnerships.

2. **Choose the Right Partners:** Collaborate with companies or individuals who share your values and will enhance your brand's reputation. Licensing is about building trust, so be selective to ensure your brand is represented authentically.

3. **Create Licensing Agreements:** Work with a legal professional to draft clear and enforceable agreements. These should define how your intellectual property can be used, the duration of the partnership, and how royalties or other payments will be managed.

4. **Retain Control Over Your Brand:** Licensing allows you to share your brand, but you still maintain ownership. Include guidelines in your agreements that protect your brand's quality, identity, and values to avoid misuse or dilution.

5. **Monitor and Evaluate:** Regularly review your licensing partnerships to make sure they align with your goals. Be proactive about addressing any issues and adjust agreements as needed to protect your brand's integrity.

6. **Set Clear Revenue Goals:** Outline specific financial goals for your licensing partnerships. Determine what percentage of revenue you expect from licensing and

track progress to ensure the partnerships are mutually beneficial.

7. **Expand Licensing Opportunities:** Consider different industries or markets where your brand could flourish. For example, a fashion brand could explore licensing for home goods or accessories. Expanding strategically helps increase your reach while staying true to your identity.

8. **Develop Marketing Support for Licensees:** Provide your partners with marketing materials, guidelines, and strategies that help them effectively represent your brand. Supporting their efforts strengthens the partnership and ensures consistency across platforms.

9. **Use Licensing to Test New Markets:** Licensing can be a low-risk way to explore new territories or product categories. Use it as an opportunity to learn about demand in different regions or industries without overextending your resources.

Licensing offers a way to monetize your intellectual property while keeping your brand's essence intact. By collaborating with trusted partners and maintaining control over how your brand is represented, you can create new revenue streams and expand your influence without sacrificing the values that make your brand unique. It's a strategy that not only preserves your legacy but also helps it grow.

BUILDING A BRAND THAT LASTS

What you're building goes beyond a logo or tagline—it's a living reflection of your vision, your resilience, and your values.

We've seen too many brilliant entrepreneurs wait until it's too late. You don't have to be one of them. Start now. Build intentionally. Protect what you're creating—not someday, but today.

The reality is that brands that last aren't just built on passion. They're built on strong foundations. This notion brings us to the next big question every founder needs to ask themselves...

CHAPTER 3

ARE YOU BUILDING A BRAND OR BORROWING TIME?

"The plans of the diligent lead to profit as surely as haste leads to poverty."
— Proverbs 21:5 (NIV)

Every founder starts with a vision to make an impact, build something meaningful, and serve with excellence. But beyond the daily operations, social media posts, and client wins, there comes a time when every entrepreneur has to ask:

Am I building this brand to pass down or to one day sell?

Either path is valid. Both are powerful. And each requires an intentional brand strategy rooted in protection.

How Iconic Brands Are Built
Think about the names that carry weight in our world today: Chanel. Ford. Oprah. These aren't just brands—they're identities. They've lasted because they weren't built in a rush. They were built with structure, vision, and strong legal foundations.

Whether your goal is legacy or liquidity, your brand must be:
- Clear in purpose
- Distinct in the marketplace
- Protected at every level

Without these pillars, even the most creative brands eventually lose their power.

BUSINESS VS. PERSONAL BRANDING: WHAT PATH ARE YOU ON?

Understanding your brand type determines the legal and business framework you'll need to build.

PERSONAL BRAND
- Built around you: your story, voice, and expertise
- Often includes your personal name, image, or signature framework
- Can be more emotionally connected to your audience
- Typically, harder to sell, easier to license or expand

BUSINESS BRAND
- Built around a company, product, or concept
- May be designed to run without you at the center
- Easier to scale, sell, or franchise

Many founders begin with a personal brand and evolve into a business brand. Both are valuable. The key is clarity on your long-term goal so we can help you legally build and protect your brand accordingly.

THE LEGAL SIDE OF BRAND STRATEGY

A beautiful brand without legal protection is like a mansion with no foundation. It may look impressive, but it can collapse in a moment.

Here are the essential legal layers we help our clients put in place to ensure their brand is truly protected and positioned to grow:

1. **Trademark Search and Registration:** Before you invest in branding, marketing, or scaling, you need to make sure your name, logo, and messaging are yours to own. A deep trademark search is the first step. It helps you avoid building on a name that someone else already has legal rights to.

Once you're clear, it's time to register your brand assets, including:
- Business names
- Logos and visual marks
- Taglines and slogans
- Product names, course titles, and signature frameworks

2. **IP Organization and Protection:** Your intellectual property (IP) is one of your brand's most valuable assets and like any asset, it needs

to be accounted for, organized, and protected. That means taking inventory of what you've created, identifying any gaps, and making sure your protection covers the full scope of your work.

Smart IP strategy includes:
- Auditing what you already have and ensuring it's protected
- Filling in any gaps where assets haven't been registered or documented
- Expanding protection across classes, business lines, or countries

When your IP is clearly organized and secured, your brand becomes more than recognizable, it becomes transferable and investment-ready.

3. **Brand Licensing:** Licensing is one of the most powerful ways to scale your brand without giving up control. Whether it's your curriculum, a program name, or a signature method, licensing allows others to use your intellectual property while you retain ownership and set the terms.

A thoughtful licensing strategy should:
- Be structured to align with your brand's values and boundaries
- Include clear royalty terms and ownership rights
- Support scalability without sacrificing quality or consistency

Licensing isn't just for massive corporations. Licensing is a practical growth strategy for founders who want to expand their impact, generate passive income, or set the stage for a future sale.

4. **Brand Monitoring and Enforcement:** A registered trademark gives you the exclusive right to use your brand—but that right means little if you don't enforce it. Owning your trademark is only half the job. The other half is policing and protecting it.

The USPTO doesn't monitor infringement for you. It's your responsibility to enforce your rights, and if you don't, it could be used against you. Trademark law requires owners to police and protect their marks. If you allow others to use similar names or branding without taking action, the USPTO (or a court) could determine that you've abandoned your rights. That opens the door for your trademark to be canceled, essentially wiped off the record as if it was never protected at all.

Failure to enforce your trademark can also weaken your ability to win future infringement cases. If you're not consistent in defending your brand, opposing parties may argue that your trademark isn't distinctive, or that the marketplace has become too crowded for your rights to be enforceable.

That's why brand enforcement isn't aggressive—it's essential.

Here's what we help our clients do:
- Monitor new trademark applications that could conflict with your brand.
- Set up alerts to detect when others start using similar names, logos, or content.
- Send cease and desist letters backed by clear legal authority.
- Resolve domain and social media impersonation issues before they escalate.

ATHENA'S STORY: PROTECTING A WELLNESS BRAND

Athena built a transformational wellness course and success followed fast. But so did the imitators. Dozens of others launched copycat courses, using confusingly similar names and messaging. Fortunately, Athena had already secured her trademark rights.

We sent cease and desist letters, shut down the infringers, and protected her market position. Today, Athena's brand stands alone—clear, protected, and future-proof.

It's a living example of why brand protection isn't optional. It's essential!

5. Website Legal Protection: Your website isn't just a digital brochure; it's a living part of your brand. It's where clients find you, engage with your content, buy your products, and trust you with their information. And just like your logo or course name, your website deserves legal protection.

If you're collecting emails, selling products, or offering services online, you're operating in a space that comes with legal responsibilities. Without the right protections in place, you could face liability for things you didn't even realize were risks.

We help modern brands protect their digital presence with:

1. **Privacy Policies:** These are legally required in many jurisdictions if you collect personal data (like names, emails, or payment info). A strong privacy policy builds trust and ensures compliance with global data laws like the GDPR and CCPA.

2. **Terms & Conditions:** These set the rules for how visitors interact with your website. They can limit your liability, outline refund policies, and define user responsibilities, all of which are crucial for maintaining control over your platform.

3. **Disclaimers:** Especially important for coaches, consultants, and service providers, disclaimers clarify what you are (and aren't) responsible for. They help reduce the risk of someone misusing your content or making false assumptions about your services.

Legal documents may not be the flashiest part of your website, but they're essential. They tell the world that your business is credible, professional, and protected.

6. Contracts That Guard Your Brand: Your brand's protection doesn't stop with a trademark; it extends to the behind-the-scenes agreements that hold everything together. Contracts may not be glamorous, but they're essential. They quietly protect your voice, your work, and the relationships your business depends on.

Here's what every growing brand should have in place:

- Contractor and employee agreements that make sure anything created for your business legally belongs to your business.
- Partnership and collaboration agreements that set clear expectations, so everyone knows their role—and what's off limits.
- Client service agreements that protect your process, clarify boundaries, and help avoid misunderstandings.

These documents do the heavy lifting so you can stay focused on building, growing, and leading. Without them, you're exposed, and your brand is vulnerable.

7. Preparing to Sell or Transfer: You may not be planning to sell or step away from your brand right now—but what you do today matters. Whether your long game is passing it down or cashing out, the value of your brand will depend on how well it's structured and protected.

If someone were to buy your business or take it over tomorrow, would they know what they're getting? Would everything be organized, protected, and easy to transfer?

Here's what makes the difference:
- A full IP and operations audit so there are no gaps in ownership or protection.
- A brand guide and systems manual so someone else can run the business without you.
- The right legal entity structure to reduce risk and support growth.
- Organized IP and revenue records that show the brand is not only strong but profitable.

This kind of prep work turns your brand into something bigger than you. Something that can be passed down, scaled, sold, or licensed with confidence.

WHAT ARE YOU REALLY BUILDING?

When clients come to us unsure of what they want for their brand's future, we ask:
- Do you want your brand to serve your family long after you're gone?
- Or do you want to position it as an asset that someone would pay a premium for today?

Both paths are meaningful. Both can change your family's financial future. However, both require an intentional legal and business strategy to get there. You're not just creating a business. You're building an asset. A legacy. A platform for whatever dreams come next. And what you protect today will determine what's possible tomorrow.

YOUR INTELLECTUAL PROPERTY FORTRESS

CHAPTER 4

THE #1 TRADEMARK MYTH THAT PUTS YOUR ENTIRE BRAND AT RISK

"An ounce of prevention is worth a pound of cure."
— Benjamin Franklin

One of the most damaging misconceptions entrepreneurs believe is: *owning an LLC means owning the rights to the name.*

Many entrepreneurs mistakenly believe that forming an LLC grants them ownership of their business name. This misunderstanding creates a serious risk to their brands. In reality, LLC registration and trademark protection serve entirely different purposes. Without a registered trademark, your business name isn't protected against competitors who can take it for themselves.

THE FALSE SENSE OF SECURITY
Registering an LLC is a smart move for protecting your personal assets, limiting liability, and gaining credibility. However, the mistake entrepreneurs often make is assuming that this registration gives them exclusive rights to their business name.

Here's the truth: An LLC only prevents other businesses in your state from using the same or a similar name. It does nothing to stop someone in another state, or even in the same state but a different industry, from trademarking your business name at the federal level. If that happens, the trademark owner could force you to rebrand entirely—even if you've been using the name longer.

THE REAL COST OF BELIEVING THE LLC MYTH

Rebranding can be devastating. It demands significant resources for new marketing materials, legal fees, and rebuilding customer trust. The financial impact is severe, and the disruption to your business can be catastrophic.

A Real-Life Example: Kosher King

Kosher King, a New York-based grocery store, invested heavily in its brand—spending $250,000 on leases, signage, marketing, and more. However, due to a lack of federal trademark protection, a Florida company with the same name issued a cease-and-desist letter. Kosher King was forced to replace signage, discard branded materials, and absorb additional costs. This situation illustrates the high price of relying solely on an LLC for brand protection.

LLC VS. TRADEMARK - WHAT'S THE DIFFERENCE?

The difference between an LLC and a trademark comes down to two things: scope and purpose.

LLC Registration:

- **Scope:** State-level protection only.
- **Purpose:** Separates personal assets from business liabilities.

o **Limits:** Does not prevent others from using your name outside your state or industry.

Trademark Registration:
- o **Scope:** Federal protection across all 50 states.
- o **Purpose:** Grants exclusive rights to use the name for your goods or services.
- o **Strength:** Allows you to stop others from using a confusingly similar name nationwide.

THE FINANCIAL IMPACT OF TRADEMARK PROTECTION
Trademarks are valuable business assets that can:

- **Increase Business Valuation:** Trademarks are valuable assets that investors and buyers look for when providing a valuation of a company.
- **Simplify Enforcement:** A registered trademark makes it easier to prevent brand infringement.
- **Build Customer Trust:** A trademark demonstrates to customers that your brand is established, credible, and here to stay.

COMMON MISTAKES ENTREPRENEURS MAKE

1. **Relying Solely on LLC Registration:** Assuming an LLC alone protects its name nationally.

2. **Delaying Trademark Registration:** Waiting to trademark until they "grow bigger," which can result in losing the name to someone else.

3. **Ignoring the Trademark Search:** Not conducting a thorough search to ensure the name is available before registering an LLC.

WHAT TO DO INSTEAD: A 3-STEP ACTION PLAN

1. **Conduct a Comprehensive Trademark Search:** Before registering your LLC, conduct a federal trademark search to ensure your name isn't already in use.

2. **Register Your Trademark Early:** Trademark registration is not just for established businesses. The sooner you file, the sooner you secure exclusive rights.

3. **Monitor and Enforce Your Trademark:** Trademarks require active protection. Set up alerts or work with a trademark attorney to monitor for potential infringements.

THE BOTTOM LINE

Believing that an LLC registration protects your business name is a risk that can destroy everything you've built. Trademarks offer the exclusive rights and nationwide protection that LLCs simply can't provide. Your business name is one of your most valuable assets. Make sure you own it.

CHAPTER 5

THE HIDDEN ASSETS MOST ENTREPRENEURS FORGET TO PROTECT

"Whoever is faithful with little will also be faithful with much."
— Luke 16:10

Can I trademark this?

If you've asked yourself that question, you're not alone.

Trademarks aren't just for big corporations or tech giants—they're for business owners who are serious about protecting their brands. Whether you're launching a podcast, creating an online course, developing a signature program, or building an iconic slogan, trademark protection is essential. If you want to be known for it, it's worth protecting.

Here's a breakdown of what you can trademark:
- **Business Name**: Your brand's identity starts here. Trademarking your business name prevents competitors from using confusingly similar names, securing your brand's uniqueness

nationwide.

- **Slogan:** Those catchy one-liners? They're more valuable than you think. If you want to be known for your slogan, trademarking it ensures that competitors can't legally use it.

- **Catchphrase:** If people repeat it, it's worth trademarking. A protected catchphrase strengthens your brand's identity and makes it easier to enforce your rights if others try to use it.

- **Program Names, Course Names, and Podcast Names:** If your signature programs, courses, or podcast names are integral to your brand, they should be protected. Trademarking these names prevents others from capitalizing on your hard work and helps build long-term brand equity.

- **Sound:** Yes, those familiar jingles can (and should) be protected. Trademarking a sound that is uniquely associated with your brand helps reinforce brand recognition. Many people don't realize that sounds can be trademarked if they help identify a brand. For example, the "ta-dum" sound you hear when you start a Netflix show and the NBC chimes are both trademarked.

- **Product Packaging:** Product packaging refers specifically to the containers, wrappers, or boxes that hold a product. It includes things like the shape of a bottle, the design of a box, or the way a product is wrapped. The Coca-Cola bottle is a great example of protected packaging. Its famous curved shape, created in 1915, is legally protected so that other companies can't copy it. This protection helps people quickly recognize the bottle as a real Coca-Cola product and stops competitors from using a similar design.

- **Trade Dress:** Trade dress includes product packaging but also covers the overall look and feel of a product or service that makes it distinctive. This distinction can include the design of a store, website layout, decor, color schemes, and even product displays. For example:
  - The layout and design of Apple stores (with their glass storefronts and minimalist interiors).
  - The decor and atmosphere of a restaurant like Taco Cabana.
  - The unique appearance of a product, such as the design of a handbag or the stitching on a pair of jeans.

- **Color:** Brands can trademark specific colors if people recognize those colors as part of the brand. For example, Tiffany & Co. has trademarked its famous Robin's Egg Blue boxes, and Louboutin has trademarked the red soles on its high heels. These colors help customers instantly know which brand a product is from.

- **Fragrance/Smell:** Sometimes, even a smell can be trademarked. Although it's rare, it's possible

YOUR INTELLECTUAL PROPERTY FORTRESS

to obtain a trademark if the scent helps people recognize a brand. For example, the Play-Doh scent is trademarked because it's so well-known and reminds people of the brand.

- **Store Design/Interior Layout**: The way a store looks inside can also be trademarked if it's unique and makes people think of that brand. For example, Apple stores are protected by trademark law due to their distinctive design, which features glass storefronts, bright lighting, and a simple layout. When people walk into an Apple store, they know exactly where they are just by the way it looks and feels. To trademark a store's design, the design must be:
    o **Unique:** It can't just be a standard layout that a lot of stores use.
    o **A way to identify the brand:** Customers should be able to tell which brand the store belongs to based on the design alone.

Protecting store design is helpful for brands that focus a lot on customer experience. If your store's look makes people remember your brand, it might be worth protecting with a trademark.

WHAT YOU CAN'T TRADEMARK (AND THE KEY DIFFERENCES WITH COPYRIGHTS)

It's equally important to understand what you can't trademark and how trademark law differs from copyright law. For instance, you can't trademark the contents of a book or a photograph. However, you can protect the name of the book if it's part of a series or trademark the name of your photography company or course.

The primary difference is this:
- **Trademark law** protects brand identifiers that distinguish your business in the marketplace. It helps consumers identify the source of goods and services.
- **Copyright law** protects the expression of ideas, such as written content, songs, photographs, and visual art. It grants the creator exclusive rights to reproduce, distribute, and display their work.

In short, trademarks are about protecting brand identity, while copyrights are about protecting creative content.

WHY YOUR TRADEMARK NEEDS TO STAND OUT

For a trademark to be registered, it must be distinctive. This means the mark must clearly identify the source of a product or service and not simply describe it. For example, 'Fresh Juice' might not qualify for trademark protection for a juice company, but a unique name like 'ZestyTwist' could. Distinctiveness helps ensure that your brand stands out and is not confused with others in the market.

SERVICE MARKS VS. TRADEMARKS – WHAT'S THE DIFFERENCE?

While trademarks protect products, service marks apply to businesses providing services. For instance, a consulting firm, marketing agency, or personal coaching brand may seek service mark protection rather than a traditional trademark. Though often used interchangeably, understanding this distinction is important when protecting your brand.

™ OR ®? WHEN AND HOW TO USE THESE SYMBOLS TO PROTECT YOUR BRAND

You've likely seen the ™ and ® symbols next to brand names or logos. The ™ symbol can be used immediately to indicate that you claim rights to a trademark, even if it hasn't been officially registered. However, the ® symbol is reserved for trademarks that have been successfully registered with the USPTO. Proper use of these symbols can enhance the legitimacy of your brand and deter potential infringers.

TRADEMARK MISTAKES THAT CAN COST YOU BIG

Many business owners fall into traps that can delay or jeopardize their trademark protection. One of the most common mistakes is failing to conduct a comprehensive trademark search before filing, leading to conflicts with existing trademarks. Additionally, choosing overly broad or too narrow categories for your trademark application can limit your protection. Careful planning and professional guidance can help you avoid these costly errors.

Imagine spending years building your brand, only to find out someone else trademarked your name last month. Now you're faced with tough decisions: rebrand, negotiate, or risk operating without legal protection.

We've worked with clients who learned this lesson the hard way. One of our clients built a thriving art business, teaching other entrepreneurs how to grow and scale their art business. When she was ready to trademark it, we discovered someone else had already filed for it. She ultimately decided to negotiate a coexistence agreement with the trademark owner. Interestingly, both entrepreneurs were artists who offered art workshops, which allowed them to carve out separate spaces for their businesses while maintaining their shared passion.

This story is a reminder of why protecting your brand early is so important. While coexistence agreements can work out, they often come with compromises that might not align with the vision you've worked so hard to build. By taking proactive steps to secure your trademark, you're protecting the countless hours you've poured into your business.

The Takeaway
Trademarking early can save you from a lot of headaches. The process isn't about timing; it's about who files first. The United States Patent and Trademark Office doesn't care how long you've been using your brand name – they care about who gets the application submitted first.

If you're wondering if now is the time to trademark, the answer is yes. Whether it's a sound, logo, or slogan, protecting your brand now gives you the freedom to grow without fear of someone else swooping in. If you need guidance or have questions, we're here to help you navigate the process.

.

CHAPTER 6

THE PRICE OF PROCRASTINATION WHAT WAITING COULD REALLY COST YOUR BRAND

"The prudent see danger and take refuge, but the simple keep going and pay the penalty."
—Proverbs 27:12

As a business owner, especially one operating in the digital space, you're constantly flooded with advice, including legal guidance. It's a lot to take in, and the truth is that much of it comes from fellow business owners who may not be at the same stage of growth as you. You'll hear things like, "It's fine to wait before starting the trademark process." But is it really?

The "I Can't Afford It Right Now" Myth

The owner of a kosher grocery store in New York learned this lesson the hard way. After opening his store on a Sunday, he received a cease-and-desist letter two days later from a Florida-based company.

The problem?

He opened his brick-and-mortar without a proper trademark search to confirm the name was available. You can imagine his shock when he had to remove part of his storefront signage and marketing pamphlets and lose the name recognition he had started to build.

Like many business owners, he believed waiting would save money, but it ended up costing him far more.

The truth is, you can't afford not to trademark. Waiting to begin the trademark process can end up costing you far more in the long run.

If another business registers a similar name or logo while you're waiting, you could face legal battles ranging from $10,000 to $100,000 (or more), rebranding expenses starting at $5,000, or even lose the rights to the brand you've worked so hard to build.

Investing in trademark protection early on prevents future risks and, in the end, saves you money by doing things right from the start.

THE "I DID A GOOGLE SEARCH, SO I'M SAFE" LIE
"I did a Google search, and no one else is using my name, so I'm safe."

False.

If you're not a trademark lawyer experienced in conducting comprehensive searches, you're probably missing some pretty important details.

A quick Google search won't show you everything you need to know. It won't tell you if someone already owns the rights to a name through a registered trademark, if they've applied for one, or if they've been using it in business without registering it. These hidden problems can cause big trouble later. That's why you need a trademark attorney to conduct a thorough, careful search so you can feel confident that your brand is safe.

Now, let's say you go a step further and use the USPTO's official search tool, TESS. While that might seem more reliable, it's far from foolproof. TESS is extremely literal; it only returns results that closely match the exact terms you enter. Even with some improvements over the years, the system still has limitations. Relying solely on this kind of search can be risky. Most people miss certain things when they try to navigate it on their own.

NAME VARIATIONS
You'll need to search more than just your exact brand name. That means looking up different spellings, abbreviations, phonetic equivalents, and even foreign translations. Trademarks can be denied if they sound similar or convey the same meaning—even if the spelling is completely different.

DESIGN MARKS (LOGOS)
If your brand includes a logo, you're not off the hook. You'll need to search by design codes in the USPTO database. This isn't a basic keyword search. It requires understanding how the USPTO classifies visual elements. And let's be honest, this part can get complicated fast.

SIMILAR GOODS OR SERVICES

It's not only about whether the exact name exists. You need to check if any trademarks are being used for similar or related products and services. Even a name that's somewhat close—if it overlaps in industry—can pose a legal risk.

COMMON LAW RIGHTS

Here's a big one people often overlook: many businesses hold trademark rights without ever registering with the USPTO. That means a simple Google search won't cut it. You'll need to dig into state registries, local business directories, social media, and industry-specific platforms to uncover these "common law" trademarks.

PENDING APPLICATIONS

A mark doesn't have to be registered to get in your way. Pending applications—those still under review—can block your own filing or cause future issues. It's like showing up to claim your seat and realizing someone else already put their name on it.

ACTIVE LITIGATION

Some marks are already tangled in legal disputes. Knowing who's currently in conflict—and why—matters. You don't want to unknowingly walk into an ongoing legal battle.

INDUSTRY-SPECIFIC DATABASES

Depending on your field, there may be additional databases to search. For example, beauty, fashion, and tech companies often deal with niche platforms where trademarks show up long before they hit the USPTO radar.

GEOGRAPHICAL CONSIDERATIONS
Thinking about growing your business in other countries? Trademarks are territorial, which means a name that's available in the U.S. might already belong to someone else overseas. If you're planning to expand globally, your trademark search should also cover other countries.

In short, a comprehensive trademark search is like peeling back the layers of an onion—you have to go well beyond the obvious. Skipping even one of these steps can lead to serious consequences, like cease-and-desist letters or being forced to rebrand altogether. So, the next time someone says a quick Google search is "good enough," think twice—there's so much more at stake than you might realize.

THE COST OF INACTION
Even with the best intentions, waiting too long can have irreversible consequences.

Danielle, another client in the personal finance space, came back to us one year after our initial consultation. She had spent years growing her brand and finally felt ready to secure her trademark. But when we ran a comprehensive search, we discovered the name she had built her business around had already been registered by someone else.

We filed anyway, hoping there was still a path forward. However, the USPTO issued an office action citing a likelihood of confusion with the existing mark. Danielle was left with few options. She considered keeping the name and operating without protection—but that would have stalled her growth and exposed her to future legal threats.

So, she made a difficult but strategic decision: to re-brand entirely. We helped her brainstorm a new name that still honored her original mission—and this time, we secured the trademark successfully. Now, she's building on a foundation that's legally protected and positioned for long-term growth.

Her story isn't unique.

Emily, also in the personal finance space, built a wildly successful podcast that hit the #1 spot on the charts. But when she finally began the trademark process, we discovered that a hedge fund already owned the trademark for her podcast's exact name.

Emily had to choose. She could attempt to purchase the name at a high cost, risk rebranding, or operate under the radar. She chose to keep the name and continue without a registration—but that means she's now operating from a place of risk. At any moment, the hedge fund could demand she stop using it altogether.

These stories aren't failures; they're warnings about how delays can force you into tough decisions.

THERE'S NO "PERFECT TIME" TO TRADEMARK
We often hear, "I'll trademark when I'm ready." But trademark law doesn't wait on your timing. It operates on a first-come, first-served basis.

The USPTO processes applications in the order they're received. If someone else files for your name before you do, you'll be left watching from the sidelines—or worse, fighting an uphill battle to prove your rights.

And if their application gets approved before yours, your options are limited:
- Rebrand
- Negotiate a purchase (often at a steep price)
- Attempt to coexist, which rarely works unless the other party agrees

We've seen clients run ads using trademarks they don't own—only to increase exposure and alert the actual trademark holder, who then takes action.

YOUR BRAND IS WORTH PROTECTING
Your brand is the heart of your business—and leaving it unprotected is like leaving the front door wide open to copycats, confusion, and costly legal issues.

Whether it's relying on the false comfort of having an LLC, putting it off until you "can afford it," or trusting that a quick Google search is enough—these common myths can end up costing far more than taking proactive steps now.

So, the next time you think, "It's okay to wait," take a moment to really think about–is it worth the risk?

CHAPTER 7

The Trademark Roadmap: How to Make Your Brand Untouchable

"But the noble make noble plans, and by noble deeds they stand."
—Isaiah 32:8

Sofia was passionate about helping women build wealth. Through her podcast, newsletter, and financial services, she created a space where her audience could learn, grow, and feel empowered.

After investing tens of thousands of dollars into a stunning rebrand, she decided to file her trademark application on her own. But the mark she applied for had already been registered by another business in the financial services space. The USPTO rejected her application.

That's when she reached out to our firm. We crafted legal arguments and submitted a response, but because the marks were identical and both were used in the same industry, the USPTO refused to register the trademark.

To make matters worse, Sofia risked receiving a cease and desist from the trademark owner, who could argue that her use of the mark was intentional and willful, especially because she had already been made aware of the existing registration through the USPTO's rejection notice.

If the trademark owner chose to pursue legal action, they could potentially seek damages for willful infringement. This could include disgorgement of profits Sofia earned while using the mark, monetary damages for brand dilution or harm, and even reimbursement of the trademark owner's legal fees. In some cases, courts can triple the amount of damages if the infringement is found to be willful.

Now, Sofia's facing yet another rebrand—more costs, more disruption, and the uphill task of rebuilding brand recognition for a second time.

Sofia's experience is a clear warning: trademarking isn't something to wing or DIY. It's a legal strategy, and getting it wrong can cost you dearly.

The Trademark Roadmap: Protecting Your Brand with Intention

Whether you're preparing for a launch or scaling an established brand, securing your intellectual property is one of the smartest investments you can make. A trademark isn't just a formality. It's your legal armor. And like any form of protection, it's most powerful when it's proactive.

In this chapter, we'll walk through the exact steps to protect your brand with clarity and confidence— from navigating the USPTO to considering international expansion.

UNDERSTANDING THE USPTO-THE GATEKEEPERS OF BRAND PROTECTION

The United States Patent and Trademark Office (USPTO) is the federal agency that reviews and approves trademark applications. Their role is to safeguard the marketplace, to make sure trademarks are distinctive, not confusing, and don't infringe on anyone else's rights.

Here's what they're responsible for:
- Granting Trademarks: Giving legal protection to names, logos, and slogans that are unique to a business.
- Preventing Consumer Confusion: Rejecting marks that are too similar to existing trademarks in related industries.
- Encouraging Fair Competition: Making sure businesses can thrive based on their originality— not someone else's reputation.

But while the mission sounds straightforward, the process is anything but. Submitting an application without understanding the USPTO's standards can easily lead to rejection, delays, or worse, legal vulnerability.

STEP 1: START WITH A PROFESSIONAL SEARCH

The first and most important step is to conduct a comprehensive trademark search.

Before you fall in love with a name, build a brand around it, or start investing in logos, make sure it's available. A quick search on Google or social media isn't enough. And while the USPTO's public database (TESS) is a helpful tool, it doesn't reveal everything—especially lookalike or sound-alike marks that can still pose a legal problem.

WHY A PROFESSIONAL SEARCH MATTERS:
Identifies identical and similar marks, even with alternate spellings.
Reviews pending applications that haven't yet registered.

Assesses risk based on how the USPTO views related goods and services.

Skipping this step is often what leads to Sofia-style stories—costly rebrands and legal stress that could've been avoided early on.

STEP 2: FILE WITH INTENTION, NOT GUESSWORK
Once you've cleared your search, you can move forward with filing your application. This part may seem administrative—but it's actually a legal filing that should be handled with strategy and precision.

Key components of a strong application:
- A clear, accurate description of what your trademark covers.
- The correct trademark class that reflects your goods or services.
- Proof of use in commerce or a solid intent to use the mark soon.

Common pitfalls:
- Vague or overly broad descriptions.

- Selecting the wrong class (which can derail the application entirely).
- Submitting weak or incomplete evidence of use.

Think of this stage as laying the legal foundation for your brand. If it's shaky, everything you build on top of it is at risk.

STEP 3: THE EXAMINATION PHASE—WHERE STRATEGY MEETS SCRUTINY

Once filed, your application is assigned to an examining attorney at the USPTO. They'll review it for accuracy, clarity, and compliance with trademark law.

At this stage, the most common issues that lead to rejections include:

- **Likelihood of Confusion**: If your mark is too similar to an existing one, especially within the same or a related industry.
- **Descriptiveness:** If your trademark simply describes the product or service instead of identifying it as a unique brand.

This is where legal insight becomes critical. If the USPTO issues an Office Action a letter outlining concerns you'll have a limited time to respond. And a strong response often requires legal arguments, evidence, and in some cases, negotiation or amendments.

STEP 4: RESPONDING TO OFFICE ACTIONS—KNOW WHAT YOU'RE FACING

Not all Office Actions are created equal.

Non-Substantive Office Actions are usually technical fixes things like formatting issues, missing disclaimers, or clarification requests. These are generally easy to resolve.

Substantive Office Actions raise deeper legal concerns. They might allege that your trademark causes confusion with an existing one or that it lacks distinctiveness. These require careful legal argument and supporting evidence.

Responding thoroughly and on time is essential.

Failure to respond or a weak response can result in your application being abandoned, forcing you to start the process over.

Expanding Your Brand Internationally: The Madrid Protocol

If you have global ambitions or even if you're just thinking ahead it's important to consider international trademark protection early.

Here's the truth: trademark rights are territorial. That means your U.S. registration doesn't automatically protect you in Canada, the UK, or anywhere else. If someone in another country registers your brand name first, you could be blocked from entering that market—or worse, accused of infringement if you try.

That's where the Madrid Protocol comes in.

This international treaty, administered by the World

Intellectual Property Organization (WIPO), allows you to apply for trademark protection in multiple countries through a single filing.

BENEFITS OF THE MADRID PROTOCOL:
- **Efficiency:** One application covers over 120 countries.
- **Cost Savings:** Avoids the expense of hiring separate local attorneys in each country (at least initially).
- **Simplified Management:** Renewals and changes (like ownership updates) are all centralized.

But it's not a magic shortcut.

Each country still applies its own trademark laws. Some may reject your application even if the U.S. approves it. Others may require additional documentation or local legal responses. That's why international strategy should always be guided by professionals who understand both global and local nuances.

If your business model includes global e-commerce, licensing, franchising, or expansion plans, international protection should be built into your trademark roadmap, not added as an afterthought.

Learning from Real-World Challenges: Junior's Story
Junior had big plans for his clothing brand. His signature baseball cap featuring his nickname surrounded by stars— was gaining attention, and he was ready to take things to the next level. Wanting to protect what he was building, he

decided to file his trademark application himself.

Months later, he received a rejection from the USPTO.

The problem? His proof of use didn't meet the legal standard. He submitted a mockup of his logo on a website, but there was no actual evidence that the caps were being sold—no labeled products, no shipping receipts, and no packaging showing the mark in use in commerce.

That small misstep cost Junior valuable time and money. And because he had already begun promoting the brand, he ran the risk of someone else trying to capitalize on it while his trademark status remained uncertain.

Junior's experience is more common than you might think. It's why we walk our clients through every step of the process—from selecting the right specimens of use to understanding what it really means to have your mark "in commerce." When done right, trademarking protects your momentum—not slows it down.

BUILD A TRADEMARK STRATEGY THAT SUPPORTS GROWTH
Here's how to think about trademarking like a CEO, not just a business owner checking a box:

- **Search smart:** Avoid legal landmines early by doing a deep clearance search.
- **File strategically:** Make sure your application aligns with your business plans.
- **Respond decisively:** Keep your application moving with timely, thorough responses.

- **Think globally:** If expansion is in your future, protect your brand across borders.

Trademarking is about planning. It's about knowing where your brand is going and protecting the road ahead.

PROTECTING YOUR BRAND'S FUTURE STARTS WITH A PLAN
Trademark protection is foundational to building a secure and scalable brand. It protects the name you've worked so hard to build, and it gives you the freedom to grow with confidence, knowing your business is backed by real legal protection.

But here's the key: successful trademarking doesn't happen by accident. It takes planning, intention, and the right guidance.

Think of it like mapping out your brand's future. Here's what that roadmap looks like:
- **Start with a comprehensive search:** Before you commit to a name or invest in branding, make sure it's truly available. This one step can save you from legal headaches and expensive rebrands down the road.

- **File with strategy:** Every detail of your application matters, from how you describe your brand to the class you file in. A strong filing isn't about filling in blanks; it's about positioning your brand for approval.

- **Know what to expect from the USPTO:** The

review process can take months, and it's not always smooth. Be prepared for feedback and know how to respond when it comes.

- **Respond thoroughly and on time:** If you receive an Office Action, treat it like the priority it is. A strong, timely response can make the difference between approval and refusal.

- **Plan for international growth:** If you're selling or plan to expand outside the U.S., your protection should travel with you. International trademarks require planning, but they're a smart move for brands with long-term vision.

- **Stay proactive, not reactive:** Trademarking is part of running your business like a CEO. It's how you stay in control of your brand, even as you scale.

At the end of the day, trademarking is about protecting what you've built and giving your brand room to grow without fear of legal surprises. You deserve to build your business on solid ground.

CHAPTER 8

EXPANDING WORLDWIDE? HOW TO PROTECT YOUR BRAND ON A GLOBAL STAGE

"The wise see danger and take refuge, but the
simple keep going and pay the penalty."
—Proverbs 22:3

You've laid the foundation. You've protected your brand at home. Now it's time to think bigger.

If your vision extends beyond borders—and it likely does in today's digital world—you have an important choice to make.

Will your brand be ready to step confidently onto the global stage, or will it be left exposed when opportunity strikes?

Today, international reach can happen overnight. A viral post, a breakout product, or a strategic partnership can take you from a local favorite to a global contender in a matter of months.

But the same speed that fuels growth can also open the

door to serious risks. In many countries, if you don't secure your trademark rights first, someone else can, and they will. If you dream of building a brand that lasts generations, your protection strategy needs to be as bold and far-reaching as your vision.

Global expansion isn't just about reaching more customers.

It's about protecting your name, your reputation, and everything you've worked so hard to build wherever your brand travels.

WHY INTERNATIONAL TRADEMARK PROTECTION MATTERS

Imagine pouring your heart into building a brand that your customers love, only to find out that someone across the globe is selling knockoff products under your name. The damage to your brand's reputation and value can be overwhelming—and challenging to undo.

Protecting your trademark internationally is about more than stopping counterfeiters. It's about preserving your brand's identity, your hard-earned trust, and your ability to grow without fear. Here's what strong international protection helps you do:

- **Stop Infringers at the Source:** A registered trademark gives you the legal right to shut down copycats in foreign markets.

- **Safeguard Your Reputation:** Protect the credibility and loyalty you've built with your audience.

- **Simplify Market Expansion:** A protected brand makes entering new markets faster, smoother, and safer.

- **Increase Your Brand's Value:** Global trademark protection is an asset that attracts investors, buyers, and partners.

How to Protect Your Trademark Globally

International trademark law might seem complex, but with the right approach, you can protect your brand efficiently and strategically. Here's how:

1. **Country-by-Country Filing: Tailored Protection:** If you have specific markets in mind, filing directly with each country's trademark office gives you maximum control. While this approach can be more time-intensive and costly, it ensures your protection is customized to each region's unique legal system.

   Example: Expanding your skincare brand to France, Japan, and Australia would mean separate filings in each country with distinct rules, timelines, and fees.

   The upside? Strong, targeted protection exactly where you need it most. Consider this type of filing if you're targeting a few high-priority, high-value markets.

2. **Regional Filings: Smart and Streamlined:** If

you're planning to expand across several countries in one region, a regional application can save time and money.

Example: the European Union trademark system lets you file once and cover all EU member states.

Benefits:
- One application, multiple countries
- Unified rights across the region
- Easier management and renewals

Ideal For: Brands expanding across Europe, Africa, or Southeast Asia.

3. **The Madrid Protocol–Global Reach, Simplified:** For broader international growth, the Madrid Protocol is a powerful option. It allows you to apply for protection in over 120 countries with a single application through your home country's trademark office.

Why It's Effective:
- Saves time and filing costs
- Centralizes renewals and updates
- Makes it easy to add new countries as you grow

Important to Know: While the Madrid Protocol streamlines the process, every country still reviews your application under its own laws. Working with an experienced trademark attorney can help you avoid costly mistakes.

KEY CONSIDERATIONS FOR GLOBAL TRADEMARK PROTECTION

- **Prioritize Key Markets:** Focus on countries where you do business now—or plan to soon. Pay extra attention to regions known for counterfeiting.
- **Understand Local Rules:** Some countries award trademarks to whoever files first, even if you were using the name elsewhere first.
- **Check Cultural and Language Differences:** Make sure your brand name translates well and doesn't carry unintended meanings in different languages.

WHY EXPERT GUIDANCE MATTERS

Navigating international trademark law without experienced help is like sailing without a map. A skilled trademark attorney can help you:

- Create a smart protection plan aligned with your business goals.
- Navigate country-specific laws and regulations.
- Monitor for potential infringement and act quickly.

The investment in expert advice is far less than the cost of fighting legal battles or, worse, losing the rights to your own brand abroad.

BUILDING A GLOBAL LEGACY

Protecting your brand internationally isn't just a smart move—it's an essential one. It shows the world you're serious about your mission, your impact, and your future.

Here's how to protect what you're building:
- Start with a clear strategy.
- Choose the protection path that matches your growth goals.
- Work with experts who know how to keep your brand strong across borders.

When you invest in protecting your brand worldwide, you're investing in the future of your business, your legacy, and the dreams you're bringing to life. Your brand deserves to be protected everywhere.

CHAPTER 9

IS YOUR BUSINESS WORTH PROTECTING? WHY EXPERT ADVICE IS ESSENTIAL TO YOUR BRAND'S FUTURE

"Wisdom is the principal thing; therefore get wisdom. And in all your getting, get understanding."
—Proverbs 4:7

We live in a world where answers are always a click away. There are videos, blogs, and social media posts claiming to show you how to protect your business—all for free. But here's the truth: free advice only goes so far. It gives you the basics, but it will never give the full picture.

When it comes to your brand, the heart of your business, you can't afford to take shortcuts. Your brand is what people remember. It's the name, logo, and message you've worked hard to build. Would you trust a random blog post to protect all that? Probably not. That's why getting help from an expert is one of the smartest decisions you can make.

INVESTMENT VS. EXPENSE: A LESSON IN VALUE
Let's break it down.

An expense is money spent without long-term value.

An investment helps your business grow and stay safe.

Think of your brand as part of your intellectual property fortress, something you've been building brick by brick. Every trademark, copyright, or contract you secure adds strength to the walls. But imagine leaving a gate wide open simply because you didn't want to pay for the lock. That's what it's like to avoid legal protection because it feels "too expensive."

Hiring a trademark attorney isn't a quick fix. It's a powerful investment in your fortress. It's what keeps intruders out, protects your name, and guards everything you've worked so hard to build. When you invest in expert advice, you're not just paying for a service. You're reinforcing your brand's defenses so it can stand strong for years to come.

WHY FREE ADVICE CAN BE RISKY

Free tips can explain what a trademark is, but they won't tell you what your specific business needs. They can't see the big picture, and they won't be there to help if something goes wrong.

Picture this: you follow free advice, skip talking to a lawyer, and months later you get a cease-and-desist letter. Suddenly, you're spending thousands to fix a mistake that could have been avoided with expert help.

WHAT EXPERTS REALLY DO

Getting expert legal advice is like working with an architect to build a solid home. It's thoughtful. Strategic. Built to last.

Here's what real professionals help you do:
- **Know What to Protect:** They'll tell you exactly which parts of your brand—your name, logo, or slogan—need protection first.
- **Avoid Costly Mistakes:** Trademark law is complicated. One small mistake could cost you thousands. An expert helps you steer clear of the traps.
- **Create a Custom Strategy:** Your business isn't like anyone else's. Cookie-cutter advice won't cut it. A good lawyer gives you a plan that fits your brand perfectly.
- **Give You Peace of Mind:** When you know your brand is protected, you can focus on growth without fear.

THE REAL COST OF DOING NOTHING

Some people avoid hiring a lawyer because they think it's too expensive. But doing nothing can cost you so much more like losing your name, your reputation, and your customers. Is saving a little money today really worth risking everything tomorrow?

WHY EXPERT HELP PAYS OFF

Here's what you really gain:
- **Clarity:** You stop guessing and start making decisions with confidence.

- **Long-Term Savings:** One consultation could save you from tens of thousands in legal fees later.

- **Stronger Brand Value:** Protected brands are more respected—and more valuable to investors and future buyers.

YOUR BRAND DESERVES PROTECTION—NO MATTER THE END GOAL

Your brand is more than a logo or a catchy name. Your brand is the value you've created, the trust you've earned, and the vision that sets your business apart. Whether you plan to pass it down, license it, or sell it, your brand needs to be protected.

So ask yourself:

Is your business worth protecting?

If the answer is yes, then expert legal help isn't optional—it's essential. Don't leave your brand's future up to chance. Protect it with the care it deserves. If you are ready to protect everything you've built, we are here to support.

ACKNOWLEDGEMENTS

To the incredible founders for whom we have the privilege of fighting for, thank you. Your ambition, resilience, and unwavering courage to create and protect your dreams inspire us daily. This book is for you—because your legacy matters.

We are profoundly grateful to the hundreds of clients we have the honor of serving at Watson & Young. Thank you for trusting us to share your stories. It truly is a privilege to do what we do.

Our heartfelt thanks go to our exceptional team at Watson & Young, whose dedication to excellence and passion for protecting founders' livelihoods make everything possible.

And to our mothers and entrepreneurial grand-mothers—your belief in us and steadfast support have been our foundation. We are forever grateful.

AUTHOR BIOS

ZARA WATSON-YOUNG, ESQ.
Zara Watson-Young is an intellectual property attorney and co-founder of Watson & Young. After earning her law degree from Benjamin N. Cardozo School of Law, she launched her own firm in 2017 with a clear mission: to help female founders protect their brands and build businesses with staying power.

Since then, she's worked with thousands of entrepreneurs—securing trademarks, enforcing copyrights, and helping her clients protect what they've built. Her work has earned recognition from Super Lawyers and the Top Women Attorneys in the New York Metro Area.

Zara is passionate about helping founders move with clarity and confidence as they scale. She brings a strategic and practical approach to legal protection, making it easier for business owners to understand their rights and make smart decisions. Outside of the office, she's a wife, a mom, and someone who believes deeply in building a legacy worth passing down.

SEAN YOUNG, ESQ.
Sean Young is an intellectual property attorney and co-founder of Watson & Young. A graduate of Brooklyn Law School, Sean concentrated in intellectual property and media law and trained through the Brooklyn Law Incubator & Policy (BLIP) Clinic—where he helped startups and creatives navigate the legal side of innovation.

Sean has spent his career helping entrepreneurs protect their trademarks, copyrights, and contracts, with experience ranging from filings to federal litigation. He's admitted to practice in the United States District Court for the Southern District of New York (SDNY) and brings both precision and perspective to every client matter.

In 2022, Sean partnered with his wife and longtime collaborator Zara to expand Watson & Young. Together, they're committed to making intellectual property protection accessible, strategic, and foundational for business owners ready to grow and lead.

When he's not serving clients, Sean is focused on family, travel, and finding new ways to support entrepreneurs in building something that lasts.